create
and
display

Cross-Curriculum

Full of exciting activities and displays for the whole curriculum

A Midsummer Night's Dream

Ages 5–11
for all primary years

Nathalie Frost

▉▉SCHOLASTIC

Book End, Range Road, Witney, Oxfordshire, OX29 OYD

www.scholastic.co.uk

© 2011, Scholastic Ltd

1 2 3 4 5 6 7 8 9   0 1 2 3 4 5 6 7 8 9

British Library Cataloguing-in-Publication Data
A catalogue record for this book is available from the
British Library.

ISBN 9781407119175
Printed by Bell & Bain Ltd, Glasgow

Text © Nathalie Frost 2011

Commissioning Editor
Paul Naish

Editor
Janice Baiton

Project Editor
Rhiannon Findlay

Series Designer and Cover Design
Andrea Lewis

Photography
Steve Forest

Mixed Sources
Product group from well-managed
forests and other controlled sources
www.fsc.org Cert no. TT-COC-002769
© 1996 Forest Stewardship Council
FSC

Acknowledgements

I would like to thank the children and staff of Holy
Trinity and St Silas School, Primrose Hill School,
St Mary Magdalene Academy, The Rosary School
and Pakeman Primary School for their artwork,
interest and enthusiasm in helping develop *Create &
Display: Cross-Curriculum*.

Thank you also goes to my family and friends
(especially Lara Sargant, Martin Usborne, the
Blooms and Richard Reinhardt of Love Art for
Schools Ltd.) for constantly listening to and putting
up with all the ideas, paint, paper and 'creative'
mess over the years.

Contents

Introduction

Since you are reading this book, then no doubt you are busy and looking for inspirational activities and displays to brighten up your environment. The first point I will make – and I have said this so many times to friends and colleagues – is not to worry. Utilise what you have – the display space, curriculum, children's work and your imagination to create transformative displays that will fuel learning.

Create & Display: Cross-Curriculum provides ideas and activities for a wide variety of topics. The displays and activities compiled for this book have been formulated to illustrate each topic in a stimulating manner for entire classes, groups or individuals, within formal teaching and out-of-school learning contexts. Further, the activities can be realised as stated, as well as adapted across the curriculum.

Artists through the ages have drawn inspiration from every aspect of life, literature, culture, science, maths and more. Therefore images from master artists are often referred to as a starting point for display. Consider engaging professional artists to work with young people, visit local galleries and museums, and utilise internet tools to expand the resources in this book.

When planning your display, gather a range of materials, textures and objects to create interest and encourage variety within the work. As well as the more obvious display materials, such as backing paper and rolls of borders, collect a variety of different colours and textures of paper that could be used for backing. A range of textures and colours when selecting fabrics can make even the most simple of displays effective. If your backing paper is plain, then you may want to add paint to brighten it up and make it more interesting. As well as having ready-made borders, ask

create and display: Cross-Curriculum

the children to make their own. This could be done as a paint mixing session. Encourage the children to work on strips of paper and to make as many colours as they can. Keep the strips and use them to frame your display. Doodles on paper will also make interesting borders, as will old newspaper, magazines, wrapping paper and recycled materials.

Having a strong collection of display materials is necessary but it is also important to consider how to use them. Experiment with folding, scrunching, twisting and bending – the children will enjoy helping to do this and it could result in a display linked to the art and design elements of the curriculum. Often when playing around with materials, mistakes become some of the most interesting elements of a display.

Every display I have put together is only a starting point. They, of course, should and can be adapted for all ages. The important point to remember is not to worry and to keep everything bright, colourful and bold. Continue to experiment with a variety of interesting material.

As well as creating a topical display, I hope you will have made a unique piece of art for your

classroom or communal space that will uplift and inspire a creative working environment.

Nathalie Frost

The Tempest

Stories by William Shakespeare (1564–1616) have been enjoyed and loved around the world for hundreds of years. Making Shakespeare accessible to primary children can be a daunting task. The following pages look at how simple elements from his work can be brought to life in the classroom through a number of creative activities. There are many versions of Shakespeare's plays that have been adapted for children. Reading these and introducing the children to sections of the original text is necessary before attempting the following displays and activities.

The Tempest is one of the great comedies by Shakespeare. Some of the themes illustrated in the play are freedom, friendship and forgiveness. The violent storm or tempest provides great inspiration for a large classroom display.

The Tempest Display

Resources

- Large sheets of paper
- Oil pastels, wax crayons
- Chalk pastels
- Strips of shiny paper
- Paints
- Glue
- Glitter
- Junk jewellery

Approach

1 Give the children large sheets of paper. Use oil pastels and wax crayons to create marks to 'describe' a storm at sea. These could be zigzag lightning marks or wavy watery lines.
2 Provide further sheets of paper. On these, use oil pastel and crayons to create colourful swirling patterns to represent the tempest. Use watery paint in different shades of blue to go over and around the oil pastel and crayon. Add glitter and shiny paper to create a shimmering effect.
3 On separate sheets of paper, draw shells and stones in pastel shades to cut out.
4 To display, place each large piece of work (from point 1 above) next to each other and scrunch and bend the pictures so they give a 3D effect. To make a canopy effect at the top of the display, use the swirling paintings (from point 2) and make them stand out by scrunching up the paper when attaching to the wall. Stick the shells and stones at random around the display.
5 Make a border using words and quotes from the text.
6 Use old junk jewellery dipped in glitter to decorate the work. Plastic mirrors added to the display will encourage children to look and add another dimension.
7 Ask the children to draw and paint Ariel the magical sprite. Decorate the image with stars and glittery pieces of fabric.

Prospero's Spell Books

Resources

- Variety of rectangular-shaped boxes
- Paper
- Paints
- Glue
- Charcoal

Approach

1 Discuss the character 'Prospero' and what his old spell books may have looked like.
2 Cover rectangular-shaped boxes of various sizes with plain white paper.
3 Paint the front, back and 'spine' side of the boxes to create the cover.
4 Draw lines down the remaining three sides to give the effect of pages.
5 Apply charcoal to make the book look worn and old.
6 Design labels for the front cover.
7 Display the books with quotes from the play.

Stormy Sea

Resources

- Card
- Tissue
- Glue
- Shiny paper
- Glitter
- Boxes

Approach

1 Cut a large piece of card (approx 10 cm by 50 cm).
2 Draw wavy marks all over the card and decorate with collage materials.
3 Make flashes of lightning and magical stars to stick out from the top of the model.
4 Stand the model up by attaching it to a box.
5 Use strips of silver paper to represent the frothing sea.
6 These can be displayed on the wall or as a tabletop display.

Macbeth

This is one of Shakespeare's most famous tragedies. It tells the story of Macbeth, a Scottish nobleman who is influenced by his manipulative wife and the prophesies of a group of witches to commit murder in order to become king of Scotland. The play is full of atmosphere. There is some wonderful imagery to be gained from reading the story. A good version of the story for young children is *Macbeth* retold by Conrad Mason (Usborne Publishing, 2008).

Macbeth's Castle

Resources

- Roll of paper
- Sugar paper/gold shiny paper
- Paints
- Oil pastels
- Plastic roses
- Chalk
- Red paper or fabric
- Photocopied words from the story

Approach

1 Roll out a large piece of paper and ask the children to draw a castle shape on it. Encourage them to draw and paint bricks using words from the story to collage onto the castle walls. They can make individual pieces in this way to form a 3D effect.
2 Paint the sky, encouraging the children to think about the shapes that are often seen in clouds.
Ask them to make some witch-shaped clouds. These can be simple profile shapes. Look at work by the artist El Greco (1541–1614), he painted some wonderfully atmospheric skies.
3 Use red paper or fabric to create a theatrical frame.
4 Draw images of the witches and colour them with oil pastel and poster paint, then attach to the display.
5 Use plastic roses and cut-out daggers from gold shiny paper to embellish the display.

create and display: Cross-Curriculum

Mind Maps

Resources

- Paper
- Black felt pens
- Brown chalk
- Red paint
- Red ribbons

Approach

1 Talk to the children about the story.
2 Give them an A3 piece of paper on which to draw a scroll shape and to cut it out.
3 Ask them to write the word 'Macbeth' in old-fashioned lettering and to surround the name with other words that they associate with the story. Encourage them to make small illustrations on the paper.
4 Use brown chalks to smudge and rub around the words and pictures.
5 Flick some red paint over the scroll.
6 Decorate with a red ribbon.

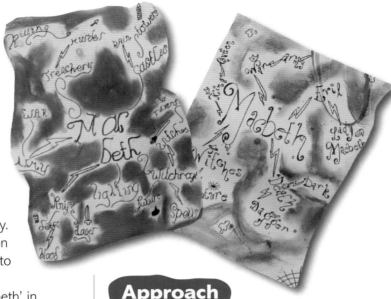

Approach

1 Discuss with the children some of the characters in Macbeth and what they may look like. Use the quote 'Look like the innocent flower but be the serpent under it' when talking about Lady Macbeth.
2 Give the children a large piece of card to draw out their chosen character. Make sure the drawing is simple (as when they have used chalk for the skin they can trace over the nose, eyes and lips with a black felt pen to make the features stand out).
3 Colour the head and shoulders using chalks, felt pens and oil pastels.
4 Decorate the image using a variety of materials, such as fabric and shiny paper.
5 Cut out and attach the image to a piece of card that will fit around the child's head.

Theatrical Head Pieces

Resources

- Card
- Oil pastels
- Chalk
- Felt pens
- Collage materials (including fabric)

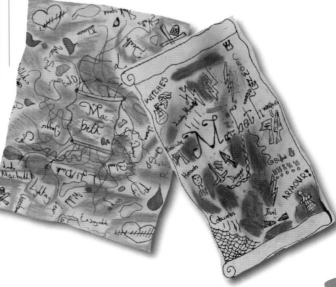

A Midsummer Night's Dream

A Midsummer Night's Dream is one of Shakespeare's best-loved comedy plays. It follows three parallel stories: four young lovers – Hermia, one of the young lovers, does not want to marry the man chosen for her by her father; Theseus, the Duke of Athens, who is preparing for his wedding day; and the craftsmen/amateur actors rehearsing for a performance to be shown at the wedding. Each story encounters fairies, mischief and fun.

Enchanted Woodland

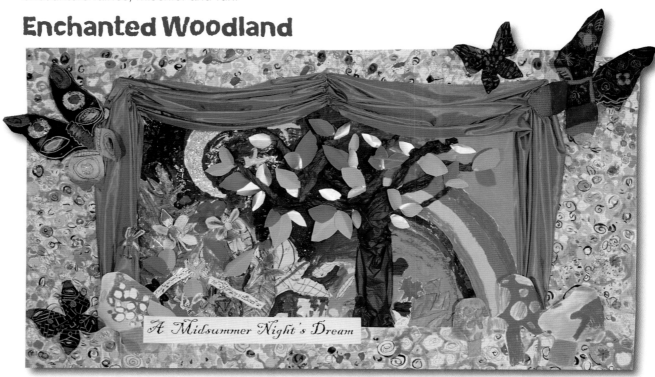

Resources

- Paper
- Oil pastels
- Perfume
- Paints
- Felt pens
- Pencils
- Glue

Approach

1 Begin with a large sheet of paper. Encourage the children to draw and paint stars and a moon to represent night. In the example, the children have shown part of the daylight with a rainbow.

2 Make a section of the picture full of greenery and flowers to represent the wood.

3 On a separate sheet of paper, encourage the children to draw fairies and colourful toadstools to cut out.

4 Draw and cut out leaves.

5 Ask the children to write some words and quotes from the play and place them among the leaves.

6 Create a giant 'bed of roses' to go around the display. Make this using oil pastels and paint. Encourage the children to fill the whole border with roses to go around the display. Use green paint in between the roses to represent the leaves.

7 Ask the children to paint a huge tree on a separate piece of paper.

8 When displaying the work, try to give it a 3D effect by folding and scrunching the paper or by padding it out before attaching the smaller piece such as the fairies, the tree and the leaves.

9 Spray the roses with perfume.

Mystical Fairies

Resources

- Craft wire
- Mod roc
- Small piece of wood
- Paper
- Fabric
- Paints

Approach

1 Encourage the children to look at each other's bodies as they move around and make sketches of the shapes their bodies make.
2 Find information and images of fairies and talk about the way they look.
3 Use craft wire to make the frame for a fairy. Attach it to a small piece of wood to form a base.
4 Cover the frame with mod roc.
5 When dry, paint the fairy and dress it using paper and fabric to make its clothes and wings.

Puck's Headdress and Ears

Resources

- Card
- Paper
- Felt pens
- Oil pastels
- Twigs
- Tape
- Glue

Approach

1 Encourage the children to draw, colour and to cut out leaves and twigs (if possible, use real twigs). On some of the leaves, ask the children to write words and quotes from the play.
2 Draw two fairy ears, then colour and cut them out.
3 Take a band of card and form a ring to fit around a child's head.
4 Attach the ears, leaves and twigs to form a headdress.

The Tiger Who Came to Tea

The Tiger Who Came to Tea was written and illustrated by Judith Kerr (HarperCollins, 2008). Her inspiration stemmed from conversations with her young daughter. The story tells of a mother and a young girl at home. They are interrupted by a knock on the door and find a tiger that promptly joins them for tea. He eats and drinks everything and, after doing so, leaves never to return again. The book can be used for all year groups. It can inspire a learning environment, such as a book corner or a writing area for the very young, or activities, such as product and package design for older children.

Creating a Story-Inspired Area

Resources

- Copy of *The Tiger Who Came to Tea*
- Paper
- Paints
- Old food packets
- Box

Approach

1 Begin by reading the story to the children and encouraging them to really look at the illustrations. Discuss the patterns and colour that have been used.
2 Ask the children to paint the patterns that they can see.
3 Work with children to create a giant tiger.
4 Invite the children to paint and to draw the food that appears in the story and any they may have at home that the tiger may have wanted to eat had he visited them.

5 Make a cupboard by painting an old box and fill it with old food packets.
6 Make labels for the display with the children in the same style that the illustrator has used on the final page (handwritten and not in a straight line).

Packaging Box Collage

Resources

- Packaging and labels (recycle old food magazines)
- Paper
- Felt pens
- Pencils
- Scissors
- Glue
- Paints and brushes
- Boxes

Approach

1 Examine different packaging with the children and ask them to design their own packets and labels.
2 Cut out a rectangular shape from a box for each child. This will form a frame.
3 Ask the children to decorate the inside of the box with cut-out packaging and their own designs.
4 Paint the outside of the box with designs based on the illustrations from the story.
5 Display your boxes together in a prominent position. You could even create a 'supermarket' corner or area.

Tiger Food

Resources

- Felt pens
- Paper
- Foil
- Acrylic paint
- Card
- Glue
- Clay

Approach

1 Look at the packaging design for tiger food in the book. Talk about how it could be made more effective to look at and to read.
2 Ask the children to make their own tiger packaging labels using felt pens.
3 Roll the card into a cylinder shape to form the tin.
4 Glue the label to the card.
5 Use foil for the lid.
6 Use self-drying clay and paint to create what the food may look like.

Alice in Wonderland

The English author Lewis Carroll (1832–98) wrote *Alice in Wonderland* in 1865 (Penguin, 2007). The famous story tells of a little girl's adventures to a magical place. She arrives at her destination after following a busy white rabbit. Alice goes on to meet a host of peculiar and colourful characters. The story can be enjoyed by all ages.

Teapots

Resources

- Copy of *Alice in Wonderland*
- Pens
- Pencils
- Paints
- Card
- Paper
- Glue

Approach

1 Read the chapter about the Mad Hatter's tea party from *Alice in Wonderland* and discuss it with the class.
2 Give the children a piece of card and ask them to draw a teapot. Cut out the shape. It may be preferable to give very young children a template of a teapot, but wherever possible encourage them to draw their own, as the finished result will be much more interesting and individual.
3 Give the children a circle of plain paper and ask them to draw or write about the party.
4 Paint the teapot.
5 Stick the circle to the teapot.

6 The teapots can be displayed on a wall display, or attach a few together to form a wall hanging or stand them up by sticking a roll of card to each piece of work as a support.
7 To make an interesting border, the children can draw and paint playing cards and the story characters. Cut around them and attach as a border for your display.

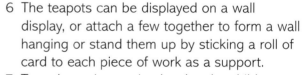

Paper Characters

Resources

- Card
- Paper
- Tape
- Collage materials
- Glue

Approach

1 Ask the children to decide which character they would like to make and then make drawings and notes describing what the character will look like.

2 Roll a piece of card into a tube shape and secure with tape.

3 From another piece of card, cut out two arms and a head and attach them to the cone.

4 Use drawings and collage materials to complete the model.

Keys

Resources

- Card
- Paints
- Glue
- Pencils
- Glitter

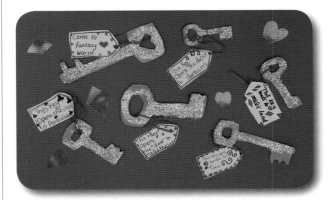

Approach

1 Use card to draw and cut out keys of different sizes.

2 Paint the keys with metallic paint and decorate with glitter.

3 Attach a label describing what the key might open.

From a Railway Carriage

Robert Balfour Louis Stevenson (1850–94) was a novelist, poet and travel writer. His poem 'From a Railway Carriage' illustrates the excitement of a child when traveling on a fast train. When the poem is read aloud, it has the rhythm of a steam train.

Faster than fairies, faster than witches,
Bridges and houses, hedges and ditches;
And charging along like troops in a battle
All through the meadows the horses and cattle:
All of the sights of the hill and the plain
Fly as thick as driving rain;
And ever again, in the wink of an eye,
Painted stations whistle by.

Here is a child who clambers and scrambles,
All by himself and gathering brambles;
Here is a tramp who stands and gazes;
And here is the green for stringing the daisies!
Here is a cart runaway in the road
Lumping along with man and load;
And here is a mill, and there is a river:
Each a glimpse and gone forever!

Painted Signs

Resources

- Card
- Paints
- Pens
- Boxes
- Plasticine
- Copy of 'From a railway Carriage'

Approach

1 Read and discuss the poem with the class.
2 Ask the children to talk about and recall stations that may be in the area or that they may have visited.
3 Draw, paint and decorate signs in different shapes.
4 Attach the signs to painted cardboard tubes.
5 Train stations are, of course, found in all different environments. To illustrate this, paint old boxes to represent bricks in a built up area and make grass from green card to show a rural area.
6 Stand the signs in between the bricks and grass by using plasticine to weight them at the base of the tube.

Looking Out

Resources

- Card
- Pencils
- Paints
- Tape
- Glue

Approach

1 Ask the children to draw and paint the back of a person's head and shoulders onto a piece of card.
2 On an A3 piece of card, draw and paint a picture to illustrate the poem.
3 Make a frame for the picture using strips of card.
4 Attach the head and shoulders using card to make them stand away from the A3 painting.

Words in Steam

Resources

- Paper
- Chalk pastels
- Fabric
- Pencils
- Felt pens
- Cotton wool

Approach

1 Draw the shape that steam may make upon leaving the train. Use a felt pen to write a word or phrase inspired by the poem inside the steam shape.
2 Use chalk pastels to colour the word.
3 Cut out the steam words.
4 Draw and paint the front of a steam train.
5 Cut out and display the steam words with the picture of the train.
6 Use strips of fabric and pieces of cotton wool to give the effect of swirling stream.

17

Let Us Not Forget

Reading excerpts from some of the war poets can be a good, strong starting point when approaching the subject of the First or Second World War. 'In Flanders Fields' by John McCrae (1872–1918) mentions poppies blowing in the fields. Discuss with the children how the poppy has become a symbol of remembrance for those that fought in the Great War.

In Flanders fields the poppies blow
Between the crosses, row on row,
That mark our place; and in the sky
The larks, still bravely singing, fly
Scarce heard amid the guns below.

We are the Dead. Short days ago
We lived, felt dawn, saw sunset glow,
Loved and were loved, and now we lie
In Flanders fields.

Take up our quarrel with the foe:
To you from failing hands we throw
The torch; be yours to hold it high.
If ye break faith with us who die
We shall not sleep, though
poppies grow
In Flanders fields.

John McCrae, 1915

Poppy Display

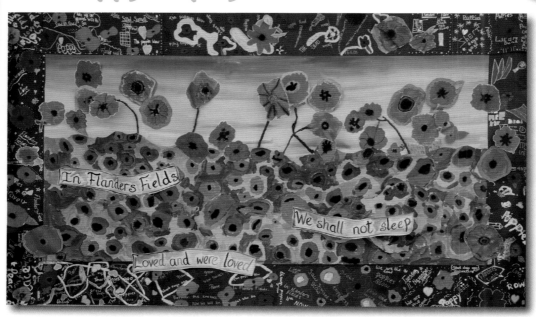

2 On a large sheet of paper, begin by making a sky background using watery blue paint.

3 Paint some simple poppy shapes. First paint the red petals, then the green grass around them, and finally, add the middle of the flowers.

4 Encourage the children to write quotes and words from the poems they have learned. Ask them to think about how the men who were fighting in the war may have been feeling and to write these words on large strips of black paper using silver or gold marker pens (or anything that will show up on black).

5 Place the black strips around the poppy field to form a frame.

6 Draw some poppies with oil pastels, cut them out and attach them to a long, thin tube of card or green pipe cleaners.

7 Attach these poppies to the display so that they stand out.

Resources

- Copy of 'In Flanders Fields'
- Black strips of paper
- Gold/silver marker pens
- Paper
- Paints
- Oil pastels
- Green pipe cleaners

Approach

1 Read and discuss the poem 'In Flanders Fields' with the children.

Medals

Resources

- Medals
- Pencils
- Paints
- Ribbon
- Craft wire
- Card

Approach

1 Ask the children to bring in any medals they may have won or been awarded and to discuss why they have them.
2 Design a medal for bravery. Encourage the children to think about positive words to inscribe onto their medals, such as *faith*, *hope*, *love* and *peace*.
3 Cut out the medal shape from card and make a hole near the top.
4 Use craft wire to make a slot for the ribbon.
5 Paint the medals.
6 Thread a ribbon through the wire.

A Poppy Wreath

Resources

- Card
- Paper
- Felt pens
- Oil pastels
- Newspaper
- Tissue/crepe paper
- Glue

Approach

1 Begin by cutting out a circle of card with a hole in the middle. Use old newspaper and masking tape to pad out the wreath.
2 Cover with green tissue or crepe paper.
3 Draw, colour and cut out small pictures of poppies and leaves.
4 Stick the poppies and leaves to the wreath.

Ancient Greeks

The ancient Greeks have always been an interesting and stimulating topic for all ages to study. The Greeks developed new ideas for science, religion, philosophy and, of course, art. They created the stories that we now call myths in order to gain a better understanding of what was going on around them. The mythical tales provide a strong starting point for both drawing and painting. When displaying work about the Greeks, it is a great idea to reference their world-famous architecture. This can be done quite simply by framing their drawings with large painted columns made from card.

Pegasus Parade

In Greek mythology, Pegasus was a winged horse. The name comes from the Greek word *pegai*, meaning 'springs' or 'waters'. Pegasus was the son of Poseidon, the god of the sea and of horses. Many of the Greek stories make fantastic displays. Simple felt pen drawings of the characters cut out and stood side by side will make an interesting display.

Resources

- Pictures of Pegasus
- Card
- Shiny paper
- Glue
- Chalks
- Oil pastels
- Glitter
- Feathers

Approach

1 Look at and discuss pictures of Pegasus. Talk about why he was different to a regular horse.
2 After practising drawing a horse in their sketchbooks, ask the children to use oil pastel and chalk to draw their horse onto card.
3 Encourage the children to use collage materials to give the horse a magical effect.
4 Cut out and place the Pegasus pictures one after the other to form a banner or a parade. If the card used is strong enough, this display will form an interesting wall hanging.

Trojan Horse

The term *Trojan Horse* comes from the Greek story of the Trojan War. The Greeks made and gave their enemy, the Trojans, a giant wooden horse as a peace offering. When the Trojans took the horse inside their city walls, its hollow belly opened letting Greek soldiers out to open the city gates, allowing more soldiers in to battle with the Trojans.

Resources

- Large box for body
- Large box for head
- 5 long tubes for legs and neck
- Newspaper
- Strips of fabric/hessian
- Red tissue
- Tape
- Small piece of white card (eyes)
- Glue
- Torch

Approach

1 Ask the children to look at images of the Trojan horse and to make drawings in their sketchbooks.
2 Begin by attaching the four long tubes to the large box for the body using plenty of tape and glue.
3 Cut a door shape in the side of the box.
4 Cut a hole where the neck of the horse will be.
5 Place the remaining long tube inside so that it sticks out and attach using tape.
6 Take the remaining box and fasten it to the top of the 'neck' tube to form the head.
7 Now use tissue or newspaper with tape to wrap around the structure. This will pad out the Trojan horse.
8 When the model is satisfactorily padded out, use strips of hessian (or other fabric) to cover the newspaper. Make sure to leave a hole in the side of the box where the door has been cut to form an entrance for the soldiers.
9 Make two eyes and two ears from card and stick onto the head.

10 Cut out four wheel shapes and stick to the bottom of each leg.
11 Give the children some card and ask them to use felt pens to draw and colour an army of soldiers. Cut out the soldiers and stick some to a tube of rolled card so they can be stood around the horse.
12 Use a piece of hessian or card to form a ladder from the middle of the horse and attach some of the soldiers.
13 Finally place a torch inside the body to enable people looking at the Trojan horse model to see the soldiers inside.

Fashion in the 1960s and 1970s

A look at fashion in the 1960s and 1970s is a great starting point when learning about these decades. Colour seemed to explode everywhere. With regards to culture and style, teenagers and young people for the first time had a chance to develop their own exciting new look.

Love, Love, Love

Resources

- Images of 1960s and 1970s textiles
- Felt pens
- Paints
- Paper
- Wrapping paper

Approach

1 Draw some love hearts in different sizes and decorate them with 1960s and 1970s style patterns. Colourful flowers and geometric black and white patterns were all popular during this period.
2 Cut out the hearts and place them together on a bright background. Use folded card to make some of the hearts stand out.
3 Make a frame for the hearts with brightly coloured wrapping paper.

Funky Clothing

Resources

- Old white shirts/dresses
- Fabric pens/paints (if the shirts are not going to be washed and are just for display, regular felt pens will work)
- Paper
- Strip of fabric for the belt

Approach

1 Ask children to design their 1960s or 1970s shirts on paper.
2 Take the white shirt (or dress) and cut off the collar. The children can then decorate it with the design they have created.
3 Wear the shirt back to front and tie with a piece of colourful fabric to form a belt.
4 Make a display from the pieces of clothing after photographing the children in their newly designed outfits.

Platform Shoes

Resources

- Images of platform shoes and patterns from the 1970s
- Paper
- Pencils
- Felt pens
- Clay
- Acrylic paints
- Varnish

Approach

1 Look at images of platform shoes and ask the children to make designs combining their own ideas with the colours and patterns they see in the pictures.
2 Use clay to form the shape of the shoe. Make sure the platform is large enough for the children's designs.
3 When the clay is dry, use acrylic paint to make the designs.
4 To give a real glossy and glamorous 1970s look, varnish the finished shoes.

The Way We Look

Throughout history our appearances and our approach to how we look have changed considerably. This section gives children an opportunity to look at the past and to compare and contrast the way people dressed during different eras. In 1941, the Minister for Labour called on women to help with the war effort. Many women stopped wearing well-styled clothing and began to dress in dungarees and headscarves. They became known as the 'land girls'. In the 1950s the 'teddy boys' wore clothes inspired by the Edwardian period. Teddy boys made it acceptable for young people to take pride in the way they dressed. They wore smart, colourful jackets and drainpipe trousers. There were also 'teddy girls' who wore very full skirts and ponytails in their hair. The 1980s saw young individuals attempting to express themselves through what they wore. Men grew long hair and wore make up and women wore bold, gaudy, colourful outfits with leg warmers.

Land Army Scarves

The Land Army Girls

Resources

- Card
- Pencils
- Chalk pastels
- Old fabric

Approach

1 Ask the children to draw a face and then add colour using chalk pastel.
2 Draw a scarf on the top of the head.
3 Use old fabric to form a knot. The scarves were usually knotted at the top of the forehead.

Coloured Coats

Resources

- Coloured card
- Paper
- Felt pens
- Glue

Approach

1 Ask the children to draw jacket shapes on coloured card.
2 Cut out the jackets and use felt pens to draw the buttons, cuffs and collars.
3 Look at images of teddy boys with the children. Ask them to draw their own teddy boy and then cut them out.
4 Place the teddy boys and jacket designs on a large piece of card decorated with musical notes.

Big Word T-Shirts and Leg Warmers

Resources

- Paper
- Paints (poster and acrylic)
- Black felt pens
- Old socks
- Old sweaters
- Glitter
- Sequins

Approach

1 Look at pictures of 1980s fashion.
2 Draw a T-shirt shape and paint it with bright colours. Use florescent paint if possible.
3 Ask the children to write on the T-shirt with a bold black pen. Use block capitals.
4 Cut out the T-shirt.
5 Take a pair of old socks and cut out the toe section, or cut the sleeves off an old sweater.
6 Decorate the leg warmers with paint, sequins and glitter.
7 Display the work side by side.

Here Come the Vikings

The Vikings are always a great history subject on which to base a display. They originated from the Scandinavian countries of Norway, Denmark and Sweden around CE 700 to 1100. They were notoriously fierce and threatening. The Vikings traded and raided across a huge area. Historians believe that the Viking raids were so successful and effective because they would strike without warning. Dik Browne created the character Hägar the Horrible as a cartoon strip. An interesting activity when looking at the Vikings is to ask the children to create their own comic Viking strip. These drawings could make an amusing and busy display.

The Rough Sea and the Long Boat

This will work well on a large display board. Viking long boats were around 21 metres long and 5 metres wide, with huge square sails and carved decorations.

Resources

- Large roll of paper
- Card
- Paints, particularly blue, brown, red and white

Approach

1 Set up a large roll of paper to form the background to the display. Encourage the children to paint using a range of blues as this will make the background more interesting than just using blue backing paper.
2 On a large piece of card, ask the children to draw a long boat (making sure that when it is cut out it will fit onto the wild blue background). Paint the ship with different shades of brown to give a wooden effect.
3 Paint a big red and white sail and attach it to the long boat.
4 Ask the child to draw pictures of themselves in battle helmets or take photographs of themselves wearing the ones they have made. Cut out the pictures and stick them to the display.
5 Cut out long strips of paper and ask the children to colour them to create a wooden effect to represent the oars.

Shields

Resources

- Pictures of Vikings shields
- Card or thick paper
- Pencils
- Paints

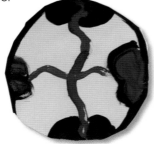

Approach

1 Look at pictures and illustrations of Viking shields with the children. Focus on simple bold shapes.
2 If the children are confident, encourage them to fill their paper with a circle drawn free-hand.
3 Ask them to draw a simple pattern on their work and then paint the shields.
4 When the shield is dry, ask children to cut it out.

Battle Helmets

When thinking of a Viking, most people will picture a fierce man wearing a hat with horns on either side. The actual Viking helmet did not have horns. From this activity the children could make either.

Resources

- Role of kitchen foil
- Masking tape
- Paper
- Acrylic paints

Approach

1 Look at images of Vikings with the children and encourage them to use sketchbooks to make drawings of their findings.
2 Wrap the foil around the top of the head. Do this several times to create the shell of the helmet.

3 Gently wrap masking tape around the foil shell so it becomes more solid.
4 Use foil to create each of the horns by twisting into cone shapes and then cover with masking tape.
5 Use tape to attach each of the horns to the helmet.
6 Paint and decorate.

Geometric Pattern

Everywhere we look we find pattern and shape. It is a good idea to collect and look at pictures, photographs and objects that illustrate this. These images can be cut out and used to make collage pictures or as part of a sketchbook activity. There are many different eras and movements in the visual art world that all use shape in a variety of ways. The Art Deco movement uses plenty of geometric patterns and is a useful period to look at when studying shape. The artist Erté (1892–1990) used plenty of geometric shape in his beautiful paintings.

Art Deco Display

Resources

- Images of geometric pattern
- Large piece or roll of paper
- Selection of acrylic or poster paint
- Squared paper

Approach

1 Look at images of Art Deco paintings and pattern.
2 Roll out a large piece of paper and select a simple image from the Art Deco Designs activity (page 29). Repeat this design all over the large piece of paper. Ask the children to take turns to draw the shape.
3 Paint the shapes using bright colours, making each large pattern the same.
4 To create a sharp contrast within the painting, incorporate a few black and white shapes. These can be made using squared paper.

Geometric Pots and Vases

Resources

- A selection of juice or milk cartons and small boxes
- White emulsion paint for undercoat
- Selection of acrylic paints
- Paintbrushes

Approach

1 Cut off the tops from the cartons and boxes into the desired shape.
2 Use a white emulsion to give the boxes an undercoat.
3 When the first coat is dry, use a pencil to draw on the geometric patterns and shapes.
4 Paint the shapes.

Art Deco Designs

Resources

- A3 paper
- Pencils
- Paints and brushes
- Silver paper or glitter

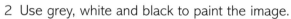

Approach

1 Using just a few geometric shapes, encourage the children to use a pencil to build up one large design on an A3 piece of paper. The designs should be very simple and should fill the whole sheet. It is a good idea to ask the children to select the shapes they are going to incorporate in their pattern before they begin. A diamond, a triangle and a circle are all used within designs from the Art Deco period.

2 Use grey, white and black to paint the image.
3 Use black in the background and leave a small white space all around the design. This will help the image to stand out.
4 When dry, use silver glitter to decorate the picture.

Geometric-Inspired Decorations

Resources

- Paper
- Paints
- Glue
- Pencils

Approach

1 Cut out four or five small identical shapes.
2 Paint and decorate the shapes.
3 Arrange them in a flower shape and glue together.
4 Roll a piece of card or paper and glue together to form a stem.
5 Decorate the stem.
6 Glue the stem to the flower shape.

A 3D Still Life

The artist Paul Cezanne (1839–1906) believed that in nature it is possible to define a sphere, cylinder and cone. Collect some images and objects that can illustrate this. This lesson can be done as an individual, group or whole-class activity, depending on how big you want the model to be. It will reinforce the idea that shape is important to artists when making a picture and that it is indeed all around us. Look at Paul Cezanne's work *Apples and Oranges* (*c.*1899) and discuss where shapes are visible within the painting.

Setting

Resources

- Cardboard box
- Acrylic paints
- Cloth

Approach

1 Cut away the sides and top of the box to form a base for the cloth and the objects.
2 Paint the box using bright colours. Try to include different shapes in the painting.
3 Use white fabric as a tablecloth.

create and display: Cross-Curriculum

Fruits and Vegetables

Resources

- Newspapers
- Masking tape
- Card
- Acrylic paints
- Plastic bottles
- Glue

Approach

1 Scrunch and twist some newspaper into sphere, cylinder and cone shapes. Cover in masking tape.
2 Paint to represent different fruits and vegetables. A cone makes a good parsnip or carrot, a cylinder could be a pineapple and a sphere could be an orange or an apple. Draw and paint leaves and stalks on card and attach using glue or tape.

Vase

Resources

- Acrylic paints
- Plastic cartons

Approach

1 Cut the top from a plastic carton and paint with white acrylic, once dry decorate the 'vase' incorporating shape into the design.
2 When all of the items are dry arrange them inside the setting to form a Cezanne-style geometric still life.

Fruity Bookmarks

Resources

- Felt pens
- Thin card
- Oil pastels
- Strips of papers

Approach

1 Give the children strips of paper as a bookmark and ask them to draw a fruit of their choice at the top and then the inside of the fruit. Use oil pastels and felt pens.
2 Fill the card by repeating the shape.
3 Cut around the fruit drawings and laminate.

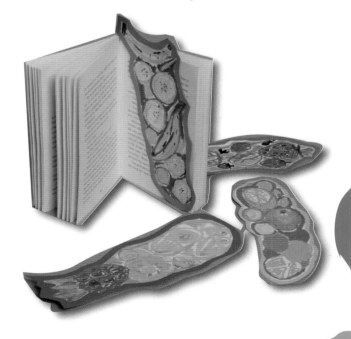

Shape in Art

This chapter looks at how to create beautiful works of art by simply using and combining different shapes. The aim is to make images that will quickly and effectively uplift and transform areas of the classroom. Look at pictures by artists Beatriz Milhazes (b. 1960) and Mark Rothko (1903–70). Compare the works of art – one is full of circles and colour, the other is a group of rectangles. They are both very different but equally as interesting. The following can be an individual, group or whole-class activity.

Circles

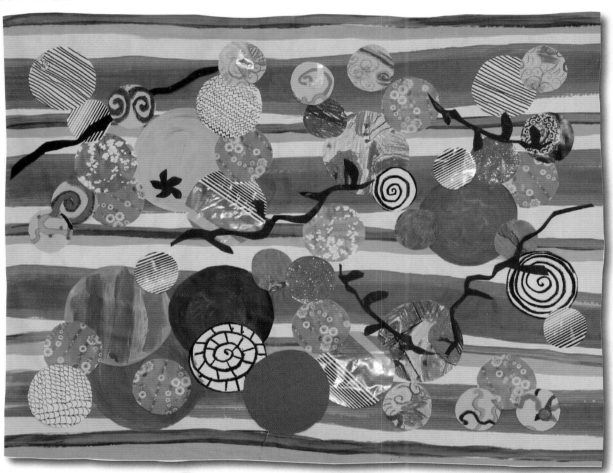

Resources

- Roll of paper
- Variety of paper types
- Pencils
- Paints
- Shapes to draw around

Approach

1 Draw and paint circles in different sizes on a variety of paper. Use plenty of different colours.
2 Cut out the circles.
3 Roll out a large piece of paper and paint in a contrasting background. This could be a row of stripes or a few giant rectangles.
4 Arrange and stick the circles onto the background to form the picture.
5 Use black paper to decorate with spirals and foliage.

create and display: Cross-Curriculum

Rothko Rectangles

Look at paintings by the American artist Mark Rothko. Talk about how he has managed to
create effective paintings by splitting the canvas into sections. Rothko's paintings are often very large –
sometimes the work is huge and dark as in the *Seagram Murals* (late 1950s) where he uses black and
maroons. Other paintings, such as *White Centre* (1950), are lighter and more vibrant.

Resources

- A3 paper
- Chalk pastels

Approach

1 Select different sets of chalk colours for each
   picture – for example, for drawings split into
   three parts use reds and oranges, and for
   drawings split into five parts use different blues.
2 Use the chalks to draw and smudge. Fill the
   page with rectangles of different sizes.
3 Give the children long strips of paper and
   encourage them to cover these in small
   rectangles to form a decorative border.

Shape Place Mat

Resources

- Thick paper for base
- Selection of different paper
- Paints
- A3 laminating machine

Approach

1 Ask the children to decide on the shape for
   their place mat and then cut it out from thick
   paper. The shape should be no larger than A3.
2 Paint, draw and cut out a variety of smaller
   shapes to stick on to the mat.
3 Laminate the mat.
4 An extension could be to design a whole set
   and even a set of coasters to match.

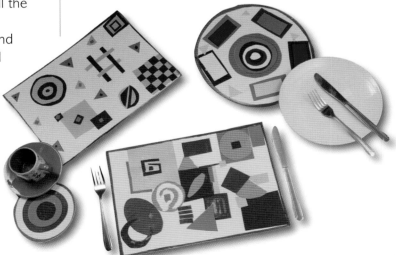

Numbers All Around

Numbers are all around us. Discuss where we find them. Where are the most unusual places? Collect old newspapers, catalogues, old packaging and magazines. Look through them to discover where numbers appear.

These pictures in this activity will be effective as individual pieces, but for a striking communal display they can be placed side by side. In this example, a variety of colours have been used, but just using black, white and greys can be equally as effective. Stick with groups of colours wherever possible. For example, reds, oranges and yellows or blues and purples will complement each other nicely. Choosing groups of colours will make the work less complicated and therefore the number patterns easier to decipher. The American artist Jasper Johns (b. 1930) made paintings using numbers. Show the children some examples of his work such as *Numbers in Colour* (1958–59). The children can then see how numbers can be used as a subject to create a work of art.

Number Pattern Display

Resources

- Paper
- Oil pastels or crayons
- Paints

Approach

1 Divide a square piece of paper into nine parts.
2 Ask the children to think of a number pattern. Use oil pastels or crayons in their chosen colours to fill the squares with their patterns.
3 Encourage the children to press hard so the numbers are bright and bold. Each number should fill the whole square.
4 Use paint to fill in the areas around each number.
5 You could also use a black and white check border to contrast with the colourful display.

Decorative Number Banners

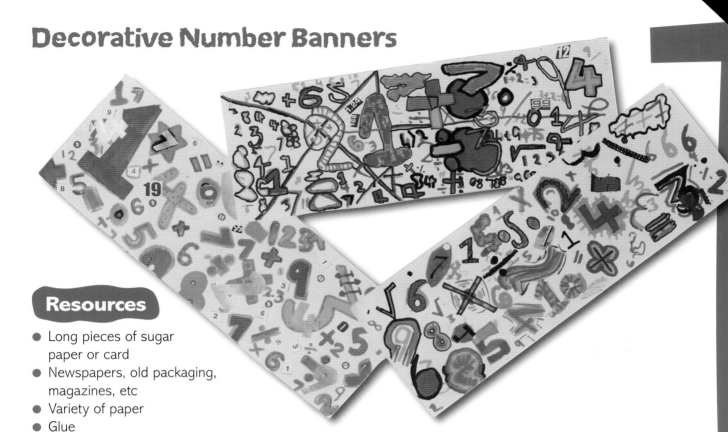

Resources

- Long pieces of sugar paper or card
- Newspapers, old packaging, magazines, etc
- Variety of paper
- Glue

Approach

1 Begin by covering the paper with different numbers and mathematical symbols. Encourage the children to make a feature of each number by making it bold and decorating it – for example, a curly number, a fat number, a spotty number.
2 Cut out and stick on numbers that have been sourced in old newspapers, packaging and magazines.
3 Cut out numbers and symbols from different types of paper such as shiny paper or foil wrapping paper to add to the collage. This will give it another dimension.

Times Table Number Bunting

Resources

- Paper
- Pencils
- Tape
- Oil pastels
- Paints
- Ribbon

Approach

1 Choose which times table you will be teaching. Give the children a triangular-shaped piece of paper – these will be the flags for the bunting.
2 On each flag, ask the children to draw and then paint the numbers for the table they are wishing to display. For example, for the nine times table each flag would show 9, 18, 27, 36, etc.
3 Fill the whole flag full of colour, making sure the number stands out.
4 Ask the children to attach the flags in the correct order along a piece of ribbon.

create and display: Cross-Curriculum

Number Box Display

This activity can easily be adapted to suit each year group. The boxes can be a variety of shapes and sizes. When complete, they make an interesting table display that can be an ongoing activity. The scrolls inside the boxes can be highly decorative, like a little treasure chest or jewellery box.

Resources

- Selection of old boxes
- Selection of cut-out numbers for collage (from old newspaper and drawn)
- Paper and pens
- Selection of shiny paper or glitter to decorate
- Varnish or PVA glue
- Paints

Approach

1 Paint and decorate a box using cut-out and drawn numbers. Each box should show a different number.
2 Make and decorate little scrolls to go inside the box. These should show problems of which the number on the outside is the answer. For example, if the number on the outside is 25, then one of the mini scrolls could read 5 × 5.
3 Glaze the box using varnish or PVA glue.

Time

There are many ways in which we measure time. A good table top display can be made by collecting objects such as old watches, clocks, sand timers and pictures of different time-measuring gadgets from around the world. The display could include drawings, models and paintings. Look at the painting *The Persistence of Time* (1931) by Salvador Dali (1904–89) as a starting point for some of the following activities. Many children may be aware of the character Doctor Who, who is known for his travels through time in the Tardis. The following activity shows children how to make their own time machine.

Time Tardis Display

Resources

- Shoeboxes
- Split pins
- Old calendars or diaries
- Paints
- Tape
- Paper
- Card

Approach

1 Talk to children about time and where we see the time written, such as newspapers, calendars and clocks.
2 Ask the children to paint an old shoebox. Make doors for the shoebox using card and tape.
3 Inside the box, paint clock faces with moveable hands. For this, use split clips and cut-out hands.
4 Ask the children to decorate the inside of the Tardis with anything they can find to do with time. Old calendars and parts from broken clocks all work well.
5 Display the boxes as shown in the picture above, on black paper painted with stars and drawings of clock faces.
6 Use scrunched up foil to form a space age border.

37

Wobbling Clock Display

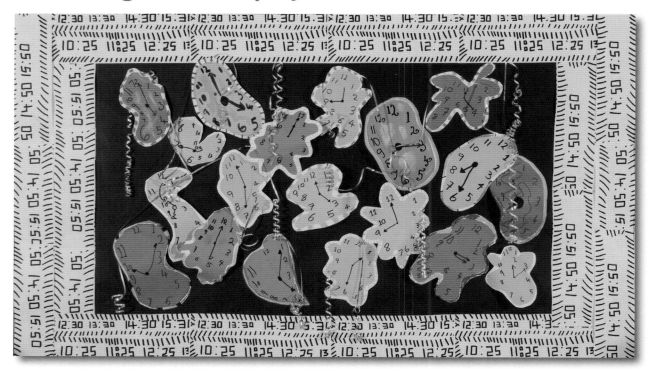

Resources

- Selection of colourful paper
- Black felt pens
- Oil pastel or felt pens
- White paper
- Roll of backing paper
- A copy of Salvador Dali's *Persistence of Time*

Approach

1 Look at the picture of Salvador Dali's *Persistence of Time* and discuss the shape of the clocks.
2 Draw the clocks in different shapes on coloured paper. Encourage the children to make their own individual clock shape. The display will be more interesting if filled with unique shapes.
3 Ask the children to draw the numbers onto the clock. Encourage them to be adventurous when drawing the numbers, such as using curly numbers, bubble writing, or Roman numerals. Ask them to select a time they wish to show and draw on the hands.
4 Stick the clock face onto white paper and cut out, leaving a centimetre or so around the edge.

5 Decorate the edge by creating a pattern using oil pastel or felt pen.
6 Put the pictures together onto a roll of paper.
7 Use the Digital Clock Strips activity to create a border to make a sharp and striking contrast with the colourful wobbling clocks.

Digital Clock Strips

Resources

- White paper cut into strips
- Black felt pens

Approach

1 Cut out long strips of paper (roughly 6 cm wide).
2 Using a black felt pen, draw digital-style numbers to represent the time. Begin to form a pattern, such as 21:10, 22:10, 23:10 and so on.
3 Decorate the edge of the paper using small marks to represent seconds or minutes.
4 Use the strips to frame the wobbling clock display as shown above.

create and display: Cross-Curriculum

Time Tree Models

Resources

- Stiff card or polystyrene board (something easy to cut, but strong enough to stand)
- Pencils
- Paints and brushes
- Cotton fabric

Approach

1 Use polystyrene sheets or card to draw simple tree shapes. Cut out the shapes and make a slit at the base. Push another piece of card into the slit to form a base to enable the tree to stand.
2 Paint the trees using acrylic paint.
3 Experiment with making wild and weird-shaped drawings and paintings of clocks.
4 Cut out the clocks and dangle them over the tree by attaching them to ribbon or by folding them.
5 The trees can be attached to the wall or will work well as a tabletop display. As well as making the trees and clocks, ask the children to paint a landscape scene on which to stand the trees.

Coasting Around

The coast remains a great source of inspiration for all types of artwork. Artists such as Matisse, Picasso and Renoir all lived on the beautiful French Riviera. Just by collecting postcards, pictures from holiday brochures, reproductions of different artists work and, of course, sketches of children's impressions of the sea you can create an effective display.

Tropical Fish Display

Resources

- Paper
- Paints (acrylic or poster, research to find or mix colours that appear common on tropical fish)
- Pencils
- Scissors
- Shiny paper
- Chunky black felt pens
- Glue
- Glitter

Approach

1 This painting could be achieved as a communal or individual activity. Show the children some images of tropical fish. Talk about their shape and colour. How does one fish differ from the next?

2 After looking at the fish, ask the children to create their own types of fish. Discuss different patterns and colours that could be used.

3 Ask the children to draw large fish, filling the paper with their ideas. Encourage them to build up the picture, placing simple fish shapes and patterns within the spaces. The more simple the shapes, the less complicated and effective their image will be.

4 Use acrylic or poster paint to colour the fish.

5 Use a separate piece of paper and ask the children to create black and white angel fish using black felt pens.

6 Cut out the angel fish and when the colourful fish painting is dry, glue them on.

7 Make a colourful border by painting strips of paper.

8 Decorate some fish with shiny paper and glitter.

Matisse Waves

Resources

- Examples of collage work by Henri Matisse (e.g. *Beasts of the Sea*, 1950)
- Different types of blue paper (it can be interesting to paint paper with a variety of different blues)
- Pencils
- Scissors
- Glue

Approach

1 Discuss the collage work of the artist Henri Matisse (1869–1954) and how he cut out simple shapes to construct an effective picture.
2 Draw chunky waves from a variety of blue paper.
3 Cut out the waves.
4 Glue the waves onto large pieces of paper.
5 You could also print wavy marks on a colourful paper to make an interesting border.

Beach Huts

Resources

- Used cartons or boxes (preferably of similar size)
- White paint for priming the boxes
- Selection of colourful acrylic paints
- Scissors
- Sand
- Tape
- Glue

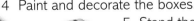

Approach

1 Look at pictures of beach huts. Discuss what they are used for and how they look.
2 Cut the top from the boxes to form a pointed shape and use a folded piece of card to create a roof.
3 Prime the boxes with white emulsion to cover the pictures and text – this will make a good base on which to paint.
4 Paint and decorate the boxes.
5 Stand the boxes side by side on a bed of sand

Surfing

This display introduces children to the water sport activity of surfing. They can make their own small surfboard displays or work as a team to create a striking classroom display. Look for images of brightly coloured surfboards and ask the children to make drawings using plenty of colour in their sketchbooks.

Resources

- Paper
- Paints
- Glue
- Coloured paper
- Oil pastels
- Shiny paper
- Card

Approach

1 To create the waves, ask the children to make wavy marks using oil pastels. Encourage them to press hard with the pastels in order to produce strong impressions.

2 Use watery paint to complete the wavy painting.
3 Glue on shiny or iridescent paper to show the froth of the waves.
4 To create the boards, cut surfboard shapes out of brightly coloured paper.
5 Encourage the children to cut out different shapes and to decorate their boards.
6 Ask the children to draw their own patterns and shapes with the oil pastels, cut them out and glue them onto the boards

Hawaiian Panels

Resources

- Large pieces of paper
- Oil pastels

Approach

1 Use oil pastels to create a pattern showing large tropical flowers.
2 Paint around the flowers using a bright sunny colour.
3 You could use the Hawaiian panels to frame the surfboard display on page 42.

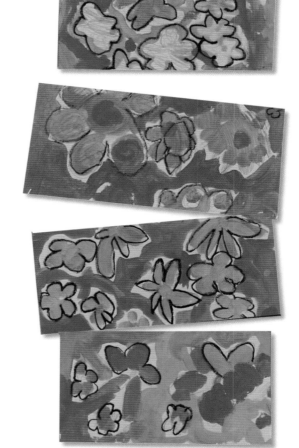

Tropical Coral Squares

Resources

- Card squares
- Brightly coloured acrylic paints (touches of florescent orange or pink can work very well, if acrylic paint is unavailable use thick poster paints)
- Coloured tissue paper
- Scissors
- Glue

Approach

1 Look at images of coral and discuss how it looks. Compare it with plants and flowers that grow on dry land.

2 Use brightly coloured acrylic paint to cover the card using the pictures of the coral as a starting point for the paintings.
3 Encourage the children to create their own different sections of coral. Will they be stripy, spotty, prickly or smooth?

All Over the World

There are so many areas that can be linked to the topic 'The World'. In this section there are activities covering the weather, travel and textiles. A quick and effective wall display can be made by collecting maps, timetables and postcards from local areas and around the world. Place them side by side and frame the collage with children's drawings of different flags. More creative ideas on this topic are explored in this chapter.

Compass Points

This activity can be made as an individual piece or as a group painting.

Resources

- Various images of different compasses
- Pencils
- Paper
- Paints
- Old maps or atlas

Approach

1 Look at images of different compasses. Discuss how a compass works. Notice how decorative some compasses are.
2 Make some sketches using a pencil. Drawing freehand will make the drawings individual and unique. Ask the children to fill the paper with their designs. Some of the compasses can show the points, others could just be patterns and purely decorative.
3 Use the drawings as a resource when creating the large piece of work.
4 Ask the children to choose a few paint colours. Explain that by being selective their paintings will be less complicated.
5 Use a bright contrasting border collaged with maps to frame the painting.

Silhouettes in the African Sunshine

Resources

- Images of the sky during sunset
- Images of Kente cloth patterns
- Oil pastels
- Watery paints
- Felt pens
- Black and white paper

Approach

1 Discuss the climate in different countries. Talk about what can happen to the colour of the sky during a sunset. J.M.W. Turner (1775–1851) was an English painter who travelled the world to paint sunsets, so using his work as a reference can be a great starting point.

2 Find out about the clothing that might be worn in hot countries. Look at images of Kente cloth from Africa and make some sketches.

3 Take a long strip of paper and use watery coloured paint to create a sunset effect. Leave space around the edge to make a frame to decorate.

4 Draw and cut out a silhouette of a person using black paper. Make the shape thin and long, like a shadow in the late afternoon sunshine.

5 Glue the silhouette onto the painted sunset.

6 Decorate the borders using oil pastels and felt pen.

7 Design sarongs, wraps and jewellery using Kente cloth as an influence for the work. Make sure the designs will fit the silhouettes.

8 Cut out the designs and glue them to the figures.

9 This picture can be made as giant communal display, but works equally as well as a smaller individual project.

Buildings and Architecture

In this section, children are encouraged to look closely at images of buildings and to examine the material from which they are constructed. Studying the shapes that can be seen in the buildings will influence the activities. The London building '30 St Mary Axe', also known as 'The Gherkin', is a glass and metal structure completed in 2004. Triangular glass windows form the surface area of the building. It is a sharp contrast to the Italian building the Leaning Tower of Pisa, which, in spite of also being a tall structure, has no glass windows; instead, each floor of the tower has arch shapes all around. Use these examples or search for interesting buildings in the local area to influence the displays.

Triangular Windows

Resources

- Images of the Gherkin building
- Pencils
- Paper
- Paints
- Collage materials
- Glue

Approach

1 Look closely at images of the Gherkin. Discuss the differences and similarities with buildings in your local area.
2 Use pencils to draw pictures of the Gherkin in sketchbooks. Encourage the children to create the pattern that is formed by the windows.
3 Roll out a large piece of paper and ask the children to make the triangular patterns using oil pastels. The whole paper should then be covered in triangles just like the surface of the building.
4 Use different kinds of blue paint, such as Prussian blue, sky blue and ultramarine to paint the triangle patterns.
5 When dry, use shiny and transparent materials to decorate the painting.
6 Use PVA to varnish the picture, as this will give the shiny effect of glass.

Gherkin Collage

- Card or sugar paper
- Collage materials
- Felt pens
- Scissors
- Glue
- Tape

Approach

1 Ask the children to draw the shape of the Gherkin on a piece of card or sugar paper. Encourage them not to make it too small.
2 Using felt pen and collage materials, decorate the Gherkin. Ask the children to use triangle shapes in their designs to reflect the idea of the glass in the building.
3 Roll a piece of card into a tube and attach it to the back of the Gherkin using tape to create a support for it to stand up.

Triangular Designs

This piece of work can be displayed on its own, but will also work well to frame the 'Triangular Windows' painting.

Resources

- Images of the building and harlequin patterns
- Strips of paper
- Felt pens

Approach

1 Look closely at pictures of the Gherkin and how the triangles form a pattern. Look at some harlequin patterns and then ask the children to use their sketchbooks to make their own drawings incorporating triangle and diamond shapes.

2 Give the children a long strip of paper and encourage them to design a repeating pattern using felt pen.
3 Display the work alongside the Gherkins or around the 'Triangular Windows' painting.

Painting Archways

It is useful to collect Internet images, photographs and sketches of the diverse shapes that we find in different buildings from all over the world. A good collection of pictures will be a useful resource and make an interesting and attractive display. It is worth finding local examples of buildings that contrast with each other. Take the children on a 'shape and structure' hunt and ask them to make drawings of what they find to use in a display.

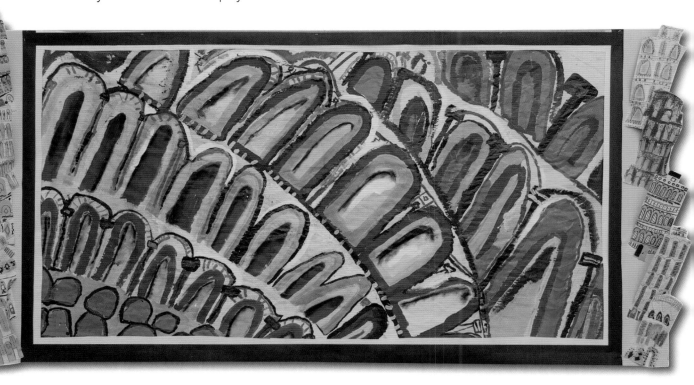

Resources

- Images showing archways
- Paper
- Pencils
- Paints
- Chalk pastels

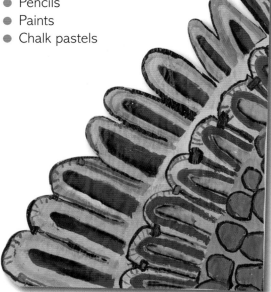

Approach

1 Look at images of the Leaning Tower of Pisa and other buildings that have archways for doors and windows.
2 Look at how the building is leaning to one side. Explain to the children that for this painting they are going to look closely at the building and fill the paper with shapes rather than drawing the whole building.
3 Place lines across the paper to represent a tier or floor of the tower and ask the children to draw the archways.
4 Paint the arch shapes using colours to represent stone and brick.
5 When the painting is dry, use chalk to add detail.
6 You can ad the chidrens' artwork from the 'Towers of Fun' activity on the next page in order to frame the display.

Towers of Fun

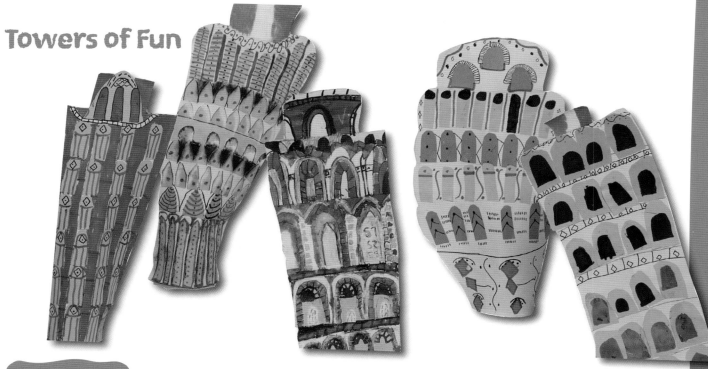

Resources

- Images of the Leaning Tower of Pisa
- Sugar paper or card
- Felt pens and pencils
- Glue

Approach

1 Use the images of the Leaning Tower as a starting point. Ask the children to make drawings in their sketchbooks.

2 Give the children long pieces of sugar paper and ask them to draw a simple outline of the tower and then cut it out.
3 Using felt pen, draw and colour arch shapes all over the tower.
4 Use cut-out archways to stick onto the building.
5 Make the towers stand by attaching them to a tube of card.

Archway Model

Resources

- Card or sugar paper
- Scissors
- Glue

Approach

1 Give the children sheets of card or sugar paper and ask them to cut the paper into strips of different sizes.

2 Gently bend the strips into archways and stick on a large piece of card.
3 Frame the 3D collage using decorated paper.

River Deep, Mountain High

Rivers form natural patterns all over the world. They twist and meander making natural works of art on the surface of the earth. Show the children images of rivers from a bird's-eye view and make sketchbook drawings from the pictures.

River Display

Resources

- Paper
- Pencils
- Oil pastels
- Collage materials
- Glue
- Selection of different paints (acrylic, poster)

Approach

1 Provide a large piece of paper and ask the children to cover the surface with drawings of river shapes. Encourage them to allow their pencils to twist and meander along the paper.

2 Complete the first part of the display by using paint to cover the rivers and land. It will make the painting more interesting if the children use different shades of blue and green. Encourage them to mix the shades they want. If possible, use a variety of different types of paint.

3 Use varied types of paper to draw, colour and cut out meandering river shapes.

4 Encourage the children to make marks that could represent moving water.

5 Use shiny paper to represent the effect of light on the water.

6 Discuss rocks and stones and where to find them. Look at the way they are formed and their different shapes.

7 Ask the children to work together on a long piece of paper to draw and paint different stones and rocks. Then encourage them to paint soil between the rock formations, trying to achieve different textures by using thick and thin paint with different sized brushes.

8 Use the river drawings to bend and twist over the river display. Incorporate different textures such as foil or fabric. Use the rock and soil painting to frame the display.

River Cones

These little models can make an interesting tabletop display. Younger children may want to use them as hats!

Resources

- Card
- Pencils
- Shiny paper
- Glue
- Paints
- Fabric

Approach

1 Use the card to make cone shapes.
2 Ask the children to draw and paint the cones to show how rivers start at the top of the mountain and flow down, curving and bending as they do.

3 Use shiny paper and fabric to decorate the river cones.

Hockney Landscape

David Hockney (b. 1937) is a British artist. Look at his brightly coloured paintings – good examples would be *The Railing* (1990) and *The Only One With Waves* (1997).

Resources

- Images of David Hockney's work
- Paper
- Paints

Approach

1 Ask the children to look at Hockney's work and to discuss what they see.
2 Give the children a sheet of paper and ask them to create their own simple Hockney-style landscape. They should consider the way roads and rivers twist and turn, and the way plants and trees can grow into wonderful shapes.
3 Invite the children to draw simple bold shapes of roads, fields, rivers and trees. Encourage them to focus on shape and not detail.
4 Use brightly coloured acrylic paint.
5 When dry, ask children to work on top of the painting, adding marks and patterns in the style of David Hockney.

Creature Comforts

Animals and birds are always popular with young children. There are so many stories about different creatures from different environments. A visit to the zoo is an excellent starting point when studying this topic. If you are fortunate enough to go to a zoo, then take sketchbooks and encourage the children to look really closely and record information about the animals and birds, noticing their shape, skin, feathers and fur.

Flamingo Display

Resources

- Images of flamingos
- Paper
- Paints

Approach

1 Look at images of flamingos, paying special attention to the way in which their necks bend.

2 Provide a large sheet of paper (the size will depend on whether the activity is for a group of for an individual) and ask the children to draw several flamingo shapes. They do not have to be drawings of the whole bird.

3 Paint a background using different types of blue to create the impression of a bright day.

4 Mix different shades of pink (from red and white) to paint the birds. It is useful to have ready-mixed pink paint in poster or acrylic, because this will vary from what the children mix.

5 Use black for the beaks and eyes.

6 You could frame the pictures with an animal skin painted border.

Blanket of Colour

Resources

- Images of animals and birds, showing different skins, furs and feathers
- Paper (squares and long strips)
- Oil pastels
- Animal fabric

Approach

1 Look closely at animals and birds either by visiting a zoo or looking at photographs and paintings. Pay particular attention to their skins and furs.
2 Give the children a square piece of paper and ask them to draw using oil pastels, noticing the patterns and marks on the animals.
3 Do not cover the whole square of paper with the same pattern; instead, let one pattern merge into the next.
4 Continue to do this until the paper is covered in pattern.

5 You could ask the children to make a zebra-style border to contrast with the wild and colourful drawings or make a frame using animal print fabric.
6 Place the drawings side by side to form a giant blanket of colour.

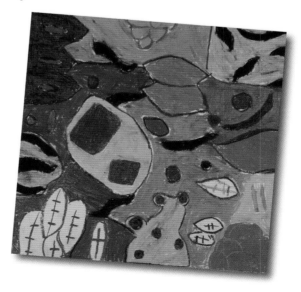

Potty Snakes

Resources

- Pots and cartons (try washing-up liquid bottles cut in half)
- Acrylic paints
- Oil pastels
- Scissors
- Glue
- Thick paper or card

Approach

1 Paint the pots with a base coat.
2 When dry, ask the children to decide on the environment they want for their snake. A jungle, a rainforest or a desert could all be perfect places.
3 Paint the pots using the appropriate designs and colours.

4 Draw and colour a long straight snake and cover it scales and diamond-shaped patterns.
5 Cut out the snake then twist and glue it around the pot.

Model Toucan

Resources

- Newspapers
- Acrylic paints
- Images of toucans
- Tissue
- Masking tape
- Fishing line
- Black crepe

Approach

1 Look closely at the basic shape of a toucan. Notice the size of the giant beak. Ask the children to twist and squash newspaper to form the body of the bird, and then make a beak in the same way.
2 Attach them together using masking tape, then wrap tape around the entire model.
3 Cut out feather shapes from black crepe and tissue paper.
4 Attach the feathers using tape.
5 Paint the model toucan.
6 Display the toucan against a colourful fabric or a painted leafy green backdrop.

Giant Palissy Plate

Many different artists look to the natural world to inspire their work. Animals, birds, fish and insects have often been the feature of some of the most interesting pieces of art. Bernard Palissy (1510–90) was a French potter whose work is strongly influenced by creatures and their habitats. Show the children some images of his strange and beautiful work and encourage them to look closely to discover the different creatures and their various environments.

Resources

- Paper
- Masking tape
- Oil pastels
- Glue
- Images of work by Bernard Palissy
- Card
- Newspapers
- Paints
- Collage materials

Approach

1 Ask the children to make sketches while looking at the work of Bernard Palissy. Notice the colours that he used.
2 Encourage the children to draw their own creatures using the same colours as the artist.
3 Provide paper and masking tape for them to make 3D creatures. This can be done by squashing and squeezing old newspaper into simple forms such as fish and snakes.
4 Cover the paper sculptures in masking tape and then paint them.
5 Decorate a large oval piece of card by drawing and painting a watery effect.
6 Attach the creatures to complete the plate.
7 Use PVA to give a shiny effect.
8 Decorate the artwork with fabric, beads and baubles.

Constructing from Nature

Looking closely at objects and examining things through a microscope can often make an interesting starting point when creating a work of art for a classroom display. Encourage the children to look around their immediate environment, using magnifying glasses to explore what they see when they look at their skin, or the fabric on their clothes or even the bark of a tree. Ask them to look as close as they can and to draw what they find. Compare the drawings and the different patterns that appear in their work. Remember the shapes and patterns that the children discover are only a starting point or an initial influence for the display. By introducing a variety of textures and different materials, a vibrant and exciting picture will be created. The examples show paintings that have been made on large paper, with children working together to create as a team, although it is equally possible for the activities to be made by individuals.

Blood Cells Display

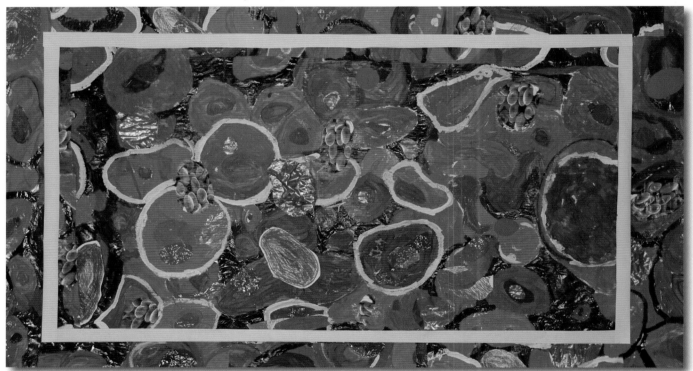

Resources

- Paper
- Pencils
- Paints
- Images of blood cells
- Tissue Paper
- Oil pastels
- Glue

Approach

1 Look at images of red blood cells in science books and from the Internet. Discuss their shape and make sketches to show their formation.

2 Provide a large sheet of paper and encourage the children to draw and to paint huge shapes to represent blood cells.

3 Use tissue paper to create a 3D effect on some of the cells.

4 Give each child a strip of red paper and ask them to cover it by drawing, cutting and sticking circular shapes to represent the cells. Use different types of paper. Print copies of pictures of blood cells and use them as part of the collage.

5 Place the collage strips around the large painting.

Honeycomb Painting

Resources

- Images of bees and honeycombs
- Paper (plain and a variety of different textures)
- Chalks
- Pastels
- Paints
- Glue

Approach

1 Look closely at images of a honeycomb.
2 Provide a large sheet of paper and ask
  the children to use oil pastels and chalk to
  recreate the patterns that they see. The main
  shape is a hexagon, so encourage children to
  make this shape and to repeat it.
3 Add paint to the drawing.
4 When dry, use different types of paper to
  stick around the shapes that represent the
  honeycomb formation.

Honeycomb Jewellery

Resources

- Colourful card cut into strips
- A variety of paper or fabric
- Velcro®
- Glue

Approach

1 Give the children strips of colourful card to
  form the basis of a bracelet.
2 Provide a variety of paper or fabric and
  encourage the children to draw long patterns
  using the hexagon shape as an influence for
  their work. Younger children could be given
  hexagonal shapes to draw around. Make sure
  the finished shapes will fit around their wrists.
3 Cut out and glue the shapes onto the bracelet.
4 When dry, laminate and fasten to the children's
  wrists using sticky back Velcro®.
5 This work can be displayed on a table or
  become part of the honeycomb painting.
  If possible, photograph the children wearing
  their jewellery and display the photos.

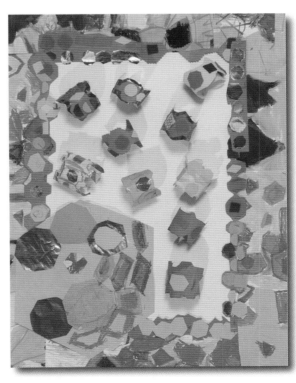

Dragonflies Display

Resources

- Craft wire
- Transparent paper
- Tissue paper
- Small paintbrushes
- Acrylic paints
- Masking tape
- Glue
- Glitter

Approach

1 Examine images of insect wings. Focus on transparent wings such as those of a bee or a dragonfly.

2 Make line drawings of the shapes found on the wings.

3 If possible, enlarge the images on the photocopier and use pale chalk pastels to give an iridescent effect.

4 Provide a large sheet of paper and ask the children to draw some large dragonfly wing shapes. Use oil pastel and chalks to make the shapes seen on the wings.

5 Introduce paint into the work. Ask the children to use a darker colour to make the lines found on the wings. It is best for the children to use fine brushes for this part of the activity.

6 When the painting is dry, glue on collage materials to give the wings a shimmering effect

7 Scrunch together some tissue paper to create the shape of the dragonfly's body.

8 Attach the wings using tape.

9 Paint the body and decorate with glitter.

10 You could add a suitable wing inspired border to your display.

Dragonfly Wings

Resources

- Images of a dragonfly or other winged insects (especially close-up pictures of the wings)
- Paper
- Oil pastels
- Chalk pastels
- Paints
- Collage materials
- Selection of different-sized brushes

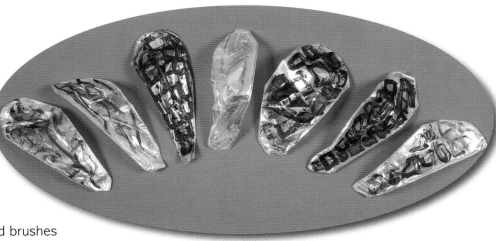

Approach

1 Use craft wire to form the shape of the wings.
2 Ask the children to cover the wire with transparent paper as if they were wrapping a present and then glue down the edges.

3 Using tiny brushes and acrylic paint, encourage the children to make patterns on the wings.

Dragonfly Hat

Resources

- Paper dragonfly
- Paper
- Drawing materials
- Green card
- Tape
- Glue

Approach

1 Give the children some green card (make sure it will fit around their heads and that it is around 20–25 cm in height).
2 Ask the children to draw reeds and grass on the card. Then stick on cut-out blades of grass.
3 Use the dragonflies from the Dragonflies Display activity opposite and attach one to each hat.

Vegetables

Examining a Cabbage

Resources

- Savoy cabbage
- Chalk and pastels
- Tissue paper
- Glue
- Large roll of paper
- Paints
- Paper

Approach

1 Ask the children to examine a variety of different leaves using a magnifying glass.
2 Look closely at a savoy cabbage and make sketches of the patterns that can be seen on the leaves. Encourage the children to make notes on their drawings that describe what they can see and feel – for example, lumpy, bumpy, curvy.
3 Provide a large roll of paper and ask groups of children to draw the veins, lumps and bumps using chalk and oil pastels.
4 When the drawing is complete, encourage the children to mix different shades of green to paint the patterns on the cabbage.
5 When the image is dry, use tissue paper to form lumps and rolled up paper to make the white veins.

Making a Cabbage

Resources

- A3 paper
- Oil pastels
- Felt pens
- Masking tape
- Chalks
- Pencils
- Newspaper
- Paints

Approach

1 Give the children a sheet of A3 paper and ask them to create some cabbage leaves using oil pastels sand chalks. They should pay special attention to the outside of the leaves and the shape these form. Next cut out the leaves.

2 To form the centre of the cabbage, roll old newspaper into a ball so that its diameter is about 20 cm. Use masking tape to hold the ball in place.
3 Paint the centre. When the centre is dry, attach the leaves using tape and glue.

create and display: Cross-Curriculum

Juicy Fruits

For this display, the children will need the opportunity to look closely at the inside and outside of different fruits. It is a good idea to obtain some of the more unusual fruits that may not be so familiar to the children. In this display a dragon fruit has been used. A kiwi fruit has an attractive cross-section that can be fun to draw and paint, and citrus fruit is always interesting to look at. The important point to remember when making this display is to use fruits that are very different in each panel. This will give the children the opportunity to compare and contrast, and will make the work of art more interesting visually. Whatever you decide to use, it is advisable to ask the children to make observational drawings before they move on to the large pieces of work.

Fruit Panels

Resources

- Selection of fruits
- Large pieces of paper
- Paints
- Oil pastels
- Felt pens

Approach

1 Select three different fruits and cut them in half.
2 Examine the centre of the fruits, paying attention to the colour and the patterns formed inside. Use a magnifying glass.
3 Ask the children to sketch what they see.
4 Roll out three large sheets of paper. Encourage the children to make a large drawing of one type of fruit for each sheet of paper, such as a kiwi panel, a dragon fruit panel and a citrus fruit panel.
5 Use the appropriate colours to complete the panels.

French

For a number of years artists and writers have lived and worked in the south of France – the mild climate and beautiful bright light have been an inspiration for many. Henri Matisse, Pierre Auguste Renoir and Pablo Picasso all lived and worked at some point in the south and today there are museums dedicated to them. Grasse is an old town north of the bay of Cannes that is known as the perfume capital of the world. The town is full of little shops selling colourful posters and images advertising the area.

French Perfume Bottles

Resources

- Images of perfume bottles
- Old perfume bottles
- Selection of empty plastic bottles
- Paper
- Felt pens
- Pencils
- Glue
- Food colouring

Approach

1 Look at pictures of decorative perfume bottles.
2 Ask the children to decide on a flower name and colour for their perfume.
3 Design a label for the perfume bottles. Use drawings of flowers to illustrate the label.
4 Cut out the label and stick it on a bottle.
5 Using different types of food colouring, mix up some perfume for the bottles. Label the colours used in French and English.

Door Signs

Resources

- Examples of decorative door signs
- Paper
- Pencils
- Watercolours
- Card
- Oil pastels
- Ribbon

Approach

1 Ask the children to decide on a room for which they would like to design their traditional French door sign.
2 Tell them the name of the room in French.
3 Give the children a piece of paper and ask them to write the word in French, making each letter as decorative as they can.
4 Use pencil, oil pastels and watercolour paints to complete the designs.

5 Cut out the design and mount on colourful card.
6 Use ribbon to tie a bow at the top of the design.

French Weather

Resources

- French postcards (children can design and make their own if none are available)
- Paper
- Paints
- Map of France

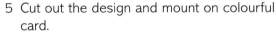

Approach

1 Make a painting of the shape of France using paints and oil pastels.
2 Make different weather symbols and label them in French.

3 Ask the children to each draw a French flag. Place the flags and French postcards around the painting to form a frame.

63

German

There are many topics that make great starting points when introducing Germany to children. The country is the home to many beautiful fairytale castles – one of the most famous and most frequently visited is Neuschwanstein Castle. This castle features in the film *Chitty Chitty Bang Bang*, and was designed by a theatre set designer during the 18th century. Germany has produced some of the world's greatest classical composers – Johann Sebastian Bach, Ludwig van Beethoven and Wolfgang Amadeus Mozart were all born there. The art movement known as Expressionism involved many German painters, such as August Macke. Children enjoy looking at work by the Expressionists as it full of strong and intense colour.

A German Castle

Approach

1 Use a large tall box as the main body of the castle and attach other small boxes and tubes to form different areas of the castle. Make sure to attach these only to the top half of the castle.
2 Paint the castle grey.
3 Make and attach paper turrets using cardboard cones.
4 Paint and label windows in German all around the castle.
5 To form the grass and trees surrounding the castles, use scrunched up paper and attach with glue and masking tape.
6 Paint the paper with different shades of green.
7 This model can be made as large or as small as wanted, depending on the size of the boxes used.

Resources

- Selection of boxes
- Cardboard tubes
- Paints
- Paper
- Card
- Glue
- Paints
- Masking paper

Expressionist Picture

Resources

- Images of German Expressionist work
- Paper
- Pencils
- Acrylic paint

Approach

1 Look at images of Expressionist-style paintings. Discuss the bright colours used by the artists.
2 Ask the children to draw a simple landscape scene containing things they may have seen on their way to school.
3 Invite the children to select bright colours to paint their scene.
4 Encourage the children to label the colours used in German.

Musical Pictures

Resources

- Paper
- Oil pastels
- Glue
- Scissors
- Patterned wallpaper or wrapping paper

Approach

1 Look at images of different instruments and draw them using plenty of colour.
2 Decorate the work with patterns. This can be done by drawing or by using patterned wallpaper or wrapping paper.
3 Write the names of different composers or instruments and place them on the pictures.

Spanish

Many famous artists were born in Spain. Collect images by Diego Velázquez, Pablo Picasso, Antonio Gaudi and Salvador Dali. Ask the children to make sketches of the works and create a colourful display celebrating the works of art created by Spanish people. Surround the sketches by making painted spotty borders.

Flamenco is a musical genre originating from Andalusia in Spain. As a dance, it is often very graceful and passionate. Many images often show women dancing the Flamenco, with their arms raised wearing very full and beautiful dresses. Red, black, white and yellow are popular colours used for the flowing outfits.

Spanish Postcards

Resources

- Pictures or postcards of flamenco dancers
- Patterned wrapping paper
- Card
- Felt pens
- Poster paints
- Card
- Fabric
- Glue

Approach

1 Look at and discuss pictures of Flamenco dancers. If possible, try to source popular Spanish postcards showing dancers with fabric skirts attached to the card.

2 Draw a flamenco dancer on some card and colour her.

3 Make patterns around the drawing using colours from the Spanish flag.

4 Decorate the border with a spots pattern. The children could draw this or stick on photocopied fabric.

5 Make and glue a colourful skirt to the flamenco dancer using colourful wrapping paper and fabric.

Matador Hat

Body Collage

Pablo Picasso (1881–1973) is one of the most famous artists in the world. He was born in Andalusia and was interested in drawing and painting from a very early age. He developed different ways of working and different ways of looking at the world. One of his major periods of work is called Cubism.

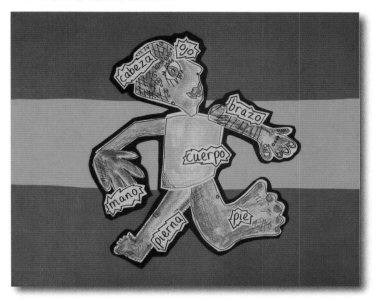

Resources

- Pictures of matador hats
- Black card
- Black crepe paper
- Gold glitter
- Gold pens
- Red tissue
- Pencils
- Glue

Approach

1 Look at pictures of matador hats and make sketches of their shape.
2 Draw the shape on black card and cut out two exactly the same size. Make sure the two pieces fit around each child's head.
3 Decorate the black shapes using gold pen or glitter. Use red tissue to decorate the side of each hat.
4 Join the shapes together at the sides to form a hat.
5 Use black crepe paper to form the top of the hat.

Resources

- Images of Picasso's Cubist work
- Paper
- Pencils
- Felt pens
- Card

Approach

1 Look at images of Picasso's work during the Cubist period. Discuss the body parts that can be seen. Encourage the children to name the parts in Spanish.
2 Draw different body parts onto sheets of paper using drawing pencils or black felt pen. Make patterns on the drawings in the style of Picasso.
3 Colour the drawings and cut them out.
4 Now have fun putting them together. This can be done as a class, group or individual activity.
5 Stick the drawing on to coloured card and label them in Spanish.

Friendship and Bullying

Bullying can be a major problem within schools. An inspiring communal display will help to reinforce the fact that both children and staff will not accept bulling and encourage those who are being bullied to know that is always best to speak up about it.

Anti-Bullying Banner

Resources

- Large roll of paper
- Pencils
- Paints
- Card

Approach

1 Ask the children to decide what colours they would like to use. Try to keep to a group of colours that will complement each other. Using too many colours may make the banner confusing and hard to read.
2 Ask the children to draw graffiti-style words that will reflect the school policy on bullying. Encourage them to make the words large and to work over all the paper.
3 Paint the words. It is always good to put the darkest shades next to the lightest. This will create a contrast and make the words easier to read.

Resources

- Paper or card
- Paints
- Felt pens
- Scissors

Approach

4 Now add anti-bullying signs.
5 Look at signs around the school and in the local area. Take notice of their shape and what they are telling or advising us to do.
6 Ask the children to design their own anti-bullying signs, making them bold, bright and easy to read.
7 Use felt pens and paints on card to complete the signs.
8 The signs will make a strong display when placed next to each other, or they can be used to frame the giant anti-bullying banner.

Sport

All around the world sport can be a way of bringing people together. Football can keep us healthy as well as encouraging people to work and to play together as a team. Often fans paint their faces to show support for the players. The flags on the drawings and masks in this display remind us that no matter where we come from or whatever our race or language, sports and games such as football can and do unite us.

Football Faces

Resources

- Paper
- Felt pens
- Acrylic paint
- Masks (these can be bought from fancy dress or craft shops)

Approach

1 Draw and decorate a face on A3 paper. Choose a flag to inspire the drawing.
2 Cut out the drawings.
3 Use a plain white mask and paint on the flag designs.
4 For the display border paint black and white hexagonal shapes to represent a football.

Every Child Matters

In 2000, the book *For Every Child* was published by Red Fox. The text is adapted by Caroline Castle with a foreword written by Archbishop Desmond Tutu. The book examines the rights of every child and is beautifully illustrated by many popular artists. It is an excellent starting point for the activities developed on these pages. The work is intended to encourage children to think about themselves and to learn to value their place in the world.

Children Around the World

Resources

- Paper
- Pencils
- Paints
- Card
- Scissors
- Paper for collage
- Glitter

Approach

1 Begin by asking the children to draw and paint figures of children using a variety of skin tones. These paintings can be simple silhouettes.
2 Ask them to create a picture using blue and green paint to represent the earth. Use old maps and different types of paper to stick to the earth.
3 Cut out a moon and stars from silver paper and decorate with glitter.
4 Ask children to use yellow, gold and orange paint and paper to form the sun.
5 Invite children to paint flags from around the world and use them to frame the picture.
6 To give the display a 3D effect, pad out the earth, then attach the silhouette paintings.

Circle of Hands Painting

Resources

- Paper or card
- Paints
- Pencils
- Hands!

Approach

1 On a large piece of paper draw a circle.
2 Ask the children to fill the space by drawing around their hands.
3 Invite them to paint the drawings of their hands using colours that complement each other.
4 When the circle is complete, encourage the children to fill the outside space using a colour paint that contrasts with the inside of the circle.
5 Use black paint to define the hands in the circle.

Colourful 'Me'

Resources

- Card
- Pens
- Scissors

Approach

1 Encourage the children to talk about themselves. Discuss their personalities and what they most value about themselves.
2 Give the children a large piece of card and ask them to draw the shape of a person to represent themselves.
3 Ask them to draw five boxes somewhere on the body. In each box, ask them to write a sentence about themselves. Make little doors to cover the sentences.

4 Use bright colours to decorate the rest of the body with their favourite patterns, colours, activities and designs.
5 For a sharp contrast, display the colourful artwork on a black and white background.
6 Encourage the children to open the doors and read about themselves and their classmates.

Painting the World

To create this design, simply find the centre of a sheet of paper and draw a large circle to represent the Earth. Allow the children to decide which parts of the world they would like to paint – for example, a desert, a city skyline or a pretty country garden. These can be painted in sections all around the Earth.

create and display: Cross-Curriculum